A Taste with a Difference
Ghanaian
COOKBOOK

2nd Edition of A
Taste of Hospitality Cookbook

MARIAN SHARDOW, MIH

Order this book online at www.trafford.com
or email orders@trafford.com

Most Trafford titles are also available at major online book retailers.

Print information available on the last page.

ISBN: 978-1-4907-9416-7 (sc)
ISBN: 978-1-4907-9417-4 (e)

Trafford rev. 03/13/2019

www.trafford.com
North America & international
toll-free: 1 888 232 4444 (USA & Canada)
fax: 812 355 4082

About the Author

Marian is a Hospitality Consultant who studied Hotel & Catering management at Westminster College, Vincent Square, London SW1. She is a Member of the Institute of Hospitality in the UK.

Marian has a Gift of Hospitality and this reflects in her generosity of sharing her cooking skills with friends and family. Marian touches people's heart with her cakes and her creative, innovative foods.

Marian is always positive and uplifting, a natural motivator and very dynamic like her Dad who gave her the best and this is the quality Marian maintains.

Introduction

A Taste with a Difference

This book is the 2nd Edition of "A Taste of Hospitality" Ghanaian Cookbook

Welcome to Ghana, the best in Africa - The Land of Smiles. The attraction of Ghana dazzles you with its delicious past and charms you with its delicious food as can be found in this book.

Through our hospitality you will discover the friendliness of our people. Revel in our music and dance and excite your taste buds with our delicious foods thereby discovering why it is great to visit Ghana.

All our people from whichever tribe cherish their traditional recipes; all these recipes make Ghanaians exceptional Africans.

Our restaurants, chop bars and eating places reflect the many cultures of Ghana and our pulsating nightlife is the hub for a perfect holiday. Ghana is a treasure house for gourmets. As you bite into these cooked recipes, you can join the people of Ghana with their passion for song and dance. Music is an important part of every Ghanaian's life and Ghana's highlife music now echoes all over the world.

Reflecting the vitality of Ghana our music, food and gift of hospitality for our traditional and modern cuisines carries forward the spirit of our continent. Good memories are made of this.

Ghana is a special Africa - A different Africa, always distinctive.

A Chat with Marian

Marian is always positive and uplifting, a natural motivator and very dynamic like her Dad the late Hon. Zubeiro Baba Shardow. Marian says:

I thank the Lord for Pastor Colin Dye of Kensington Temple who always supports me to fulfil my calling in hospitality. Pastor Colin stated that anytime he sees me he sees delicious food and this makes him hungry - WOW! What an encourager.

Thanks to Pastor Bruce Atkinson for your prayers.

Many thanks to Nana for helping to put the pieces of this puzzle together.

Thanks to Brother Kofi for your prayers.

In remembrance of our late Akora Jacob who would have been available to see this piece come together.

Many thanks to my big brother Professor Abu Shardow Abarry for always being there for me and for your input, we have always been best friends since childhood and I hope this book will take us down Memory Lane.

These Ghanaian sweets, savouries and snacks are brilliant for picnics and lunchboxes. They are for entertaining and for when you do not have time to prepare big meals when you invite your friends and family over for a quick bite. The ingredients can be purchased in African/Ghanaian Supermarkets or major Supermarkets in the World Foods section.

Gari Pudding Serves 3 - 4 People

1 egg (beaten)
2 tablespoons of Gari
1 tablespoon of demerara/brown sugar
1/2 pint milk (fresh)
1/2 teaspoon nutmeg

1. Wash the Gari and put into a saucepan
2. Add the fresh milk and boil for 20 mins stirring
3. Add sugar and allow to cool
4. Stir in beaten egg and nutmeg
5. Pour into a greased pie dish and bake for 1/2 hour
6. Serve with evaporated milk and honey

Pineapple Fritters

1 fresh pineapple (peeled / sliced)
1oz butter melted
1 egg
Brown Sugar to taste
4ozs whole meal flour
1 teaspoon baking powder

1. Sieve the flour and baking powder into a bowl to make the batter
2. Add the yolk of the egg, melted butter and 1 gill of warm water and mix together well
3. Whisk the white of the egg to a stiff froth, then fold into the mixture
4. Dip a slice of the pineapple in the batter and drop into hot fat
5. Cook until golden brown, then dredge with the brown sugar before serving

Pawpaw Fritters

1 fresh pawpaw
Brown Sugar
4ozs whole meal flour
1 egg
1oz butter melted
1 teaspoon baking powder
Water

1. Peel the pawpaw and remove the seeds
2. Slice pawpaw about 2ins long
3. Make the batter with the flour, baking powder, egg and melted butter and beat well
4. Dip the slices of pawpaw into the batter, one at a time and drop into hot fat
5. Cook until golden brown
6. Dredge with brown sugar before serving

Coconut Pie

6oz short crust pastry - using 1 1/2 cups of whole meal flour,
1 - 2 eggs
3 ozs butter
2 - 4 teaspoons sugar
1/2 pint (1 cup) milk
1/2 cup freshly grated coconut or desiccated coconut

1. Make pastry by mixing up all dry ingredients, butter and a little milk, then roll out and line a pie dish with the pastry
2. Prick the bottom and set on a basin of cold salted water till required
3. Grate coconut if using fresh coconut
4. Boil milk, beat egg lightly, add sugar, salt and stir in hot milk and coconut
5. Pour filling into pastry case, bake at once in a fairly hot oven @ 400 degrees Fahrenheit
6. Reduce heat after 10 minutes, otherwise the custard mixture will boil and curdle
7. Cook until pastry is golden brown and mixture set about 30 - 40 minutes

Banana Cake

4oz (1/2 cup) shortening (butter or sunflower oil)
4ozs brown sugar
2 eggs
1 cup mashed banana
1/2lb (2 cups) flour (preferably whole meal)
1 teaspoon baking powder
A pinch of salt
Milk to mix
1/2 cup chopped nuts (optional)

1. Cream sugar with butter / oil then add eggs
2. Add mashed banana then stir in flour
3. Bake in a moderate oven at 160 degrees Celsius for 30 mins

Yam Biscuits

1 cup of mashed boiled yam
1/4 glass of fresh milk
4 tablespoons melted butter
1 teaspoon baking powder
1 tablespoon brown sugar or honey
1 1/2 cups sifted whole meal flour
A pinch of salt
1/2 teaspoon nutmeg

1. Mix up mashed yam with the milk and melted butter and stir in the remaining ingredients
2. Turn mixture on to a floured board, knead lightly, then roll out to 1/2in thick
3. Use biscuit cutters to cut up into various shapes and place on a greased baking sheet and bake in a hot oven at 200 degrees Celsius for 15 to 20 minutes
4. Serve as a tea biscuit

Sweet Potato Biscuits

1 cup of mashed sweet potato
1/4 glass of fresh milk
4 tablespoons melted butter
1 teaspoon baking powder
1 tablespoon brown sugar or honey
1 1/2 cups sifted whole meal self raising flour
A pinch of salt
1/2 teaspoon cinnamon

1. Mix up the mashed sweet potato with the milk and melted butter and stir in remaining ingredients
2. Turn on to a floured board, knead lightly, then roll out to 1/2in thick
3. Use biscuit cutters to cut up into various shapes and place on a greased baking sheet and bake in a hot oven at 200 degrees Celsius for 15 to 20 minutes
4. Serve as a tea biscuit
5. You may omit the sugar or sweetener and use sweet potato biscuits to garnish stews

Cassava Biscuits

1 cup mashed boiled cassava
1/4 glass of fresh milk
4 tablespoons melted butter
1 teaspoon baking powder
1 tablespoon brown sugar or honey
1 1/2 cups sifted whole meal flour
A pinch of salt
1/2 teaspoon nutmeg

1. Mix up the mashed cassava with the milk and melted butter and stir in remaining ingredients
2. Turn mixture on to a floured board, knead lightly, then roll out to 1/2in thick
3. Use biscuit cutters to cut up into various shapes and place on a greased baking sheet and bake in a hot oven at 200 degrees Celsius for 15 to 20 mins
4. Serve as a tea biscuit or with juices or soft drinks

Roasted Cornmeal Biscuits

4ozs ground roasted cornmeal
2 eggs
6oz whole meal flour
4ozs brown sugar
4ozs butter
A pinch of salt
1/2 teaspoon nutmeg
Grated lemon peel of 2 lemons
Milk to mix

1. Rub fat into flour, add baking powder, sugar, salt and ground roasted cornmeal
2. Beat egg lightly, add egg and milk to make a dough
3. Turn on to a floured board, knead lightly and roll out to 1/2in thick
4. Use biscuit cutters to cut into shapes
5. Place on a greased baking sheet and bake in a hot oven at 200 degrees celcius for 15 to 20 mins
6. Serve with tea, juices or soft drinks

CORNMEAL MUFFINS

¾ cups cornmeal
1 1/4 cups whole meal flour
1 teaspoon baking powder
1 tablespoon brown / demerara sugar / honey
2 tablespoons shortening (butter or sunflower oil or olive oil)
1 egg
A pinch of salt
Milk or water to mix (Almond or Coconut milk or milk of your choice)

1. Heat oven to 200C/180C fan/gas 6 and brush a 12-hole muffin tin with some of the melted butter Put the shortening i.e. Butter or oil into a pan and heat for 5 mins
2. Mix together the whole meal self raising flour, cornmeal, baking powder and demerara sugar or honey with the pinch of salt in a large mixing bowl. Whisk together the egg, and milk, then stir into the dry ingredients and mix well.
3. Divide between the muffin holes (they will be quite full) and bake for 25-30 mins or until golden brown and cooked through – poke in a skewer to check. Best eaten warm

Basic Sweet Doughnut Recipe

75g (3ozs) Plain flour (whole meal)
50g (2ozs) brown sugar or castor sugar / Splenda sweetener
2 x 5mls spoons (2tbps) baking powder
1/4 teaspoon salt
1 teaspoon nutmeg
75ml (3fl. ozs) milk
1 large egg
2 tablespoons melted butter, margarine or oil

1. Combine dry ingredients in a medium mixing bowl
2. Add the milk, egg, butter or margarine or oil
3. Stir until batter is smooth, then deep fry in spoonfuls

Traditional Doughnut Recipe

50g (2ozs) flour (whole meal)
2tsps sugar brown
Pinch of salt
1/2 top blend dried yeast
1 egg
2 tablespoon warm milk
25g (1oz) melted butter

1. Mix together flour, sugar, salt and yeast
2. Beat in egg and milk until smooth then beat in melted butter
3. Cover with a damp cloth and leave in a warm place for approx. 20 mins (or prove in microwave on defrost for 1 1/2 mins) until the dough has doubled in size
4. Preheat deep fat fryer and spoon drop them into the hot oil
5. Fry until golden brown

Gari Buns - Makes 20 Buns

5ozs Gari – gari is made with grated cassava and then dried
it looks like couscous
5oz whole meal flour
2oz demerara sugar
2oz butter
1 egg
1 teaspoon nutmeg
1 teaspoon baking powder
A pinch of salt
A little milk

1. Damp the gari with a little water
2. Rub butter into flour, then add baking powder, sugar, salt and gari and nutmeg
3. Add lightly beaten egg and enough milk to make a stiff dough
4. Use a tablespoon to drop onto greased baking tin
5. Bake in a hot oven at 200 degrees Celsius for 15 - 20 mins

GARI AND COCONUT BUNS

3ozs gari
3ozs whole meal flour
1oz butter
1 egg
1/2 teaspoon of cinnamon
1 teaspoon baking powder
2oz grated or desiccated coconut
2oz brown sugar
1/4 teaspoon salt
1/2 teaspoon nutmeg
Milk to mix

1. Damp the gari with a little water
2. Rub butter into flour, then add baking powder, sugar, salt, gari, coconut, nutmeg and cinnamon
3. Add lightly beaten egg and enough milk to make a stiff dough
4. Use a tablespoon to drop onto a greased tin and bake in a hot oven at 200 degrees for 15 - 20 mins

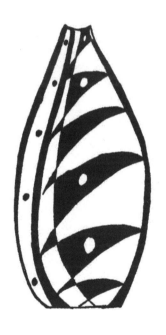

Gari And Nut Bun

3ozs gari
3ozs whole meal flour
1oz butter
1 egg
1/2 teaspoon cinnamon
1 teaspoon baking powder
2ozs or 4 tablespoons crushed nuts (of your choice)
2oz brown sugar
1/4 teaspoon salt
Milk to mix

1. Damp gari with a little water
2. Rub butter into flour, add baking powder, sugar, salt and the gari
3. Add lightly beaten egg and enough milk to make a stiff dough
4. Use a tablespoon to drop mixture onto a greased baking tin or you can use paper cups
5. Bake in a hot oven at 200 degrees celcius for 15 to 20 mins
6. Serve with fresh cold coconut water

Cocoa Chocolate Buns

5ozs whole meal flour
2oz brown sugar
2oz butter
1 tablespoon cocoa powder
1 teaspoon vanilla essence
1 teaspoon baking powder
1 egg
A pinch of salt
A little milk

1. Sift cocoa powder with flour, rub fat into it, add baking powder, sugar and salt
2. Add lightly beaten egg and vanilla essence and enough milk to make into a stiff dough
3. Use a tablespoon to drop mixture into cupcakes and bake on a baking tin for 15 to 20 mins

Baked Ripe Plantain

4 ripe plantains
1 cup of roasted groundnuts or nuts of your choice

1. Turn on oven to 200 degrees celcius and wash and dry plantains
2. Peel the ripe plantains by cutting into the skins lengthwise
3. Place peeled plantains back into the peels and bake for 30 mins to 45 mins until golden brown
4. Remove from oven and serve with the roasted nuts and a refreshing drink like coconut water or water melon juice

GRILLED PLANTAIN

4 ripe plantains

1. Wash plantains, then peel and cut into halves and slice lengthwise
2. Place onto a grill pan and grill plantains until golden brown then turn and grill other side till golden brown
3. Can be served with roasted nuts or palmnut soup, groundnut soup or any stew of your choice

ROASTED COCOYAM

2 big cocoyams

1. Wash cocoyams, peel and cut them up chunky and place on a greased baking tray then place in oven at 200 degrees Celsius for 30 mins to 45 mins until golden brown
2. Can be served with stew of your choice

Roasted Cassava

1 kilo bag of frozen peeled and sliced cassava or 2 large cassavas (washed, peeled and cut up chunky)

1. Place cassava in a hot oven at 200 degrees celcius for 30 mins to 45 minutes until golden brown
2. Serve with spinach stew, palaver sauce (recipe in my other cookbook - A Taste of Hospitality)

Cocoyam Chips

2 big cocoyams
All seasoning
1/2 pint coconut oil

1. Wash cocoyams, peel and cut them into chunky chips
2. Deep fry in coconut oil until golden brown, remove and drain fat by placing chips in a seize or on paper towel
3. Sprinkle the All seasoning sparingly onto cocoyams chips
4. Serve with stew or sauce of your choice

CORN BREAD SERVES 6

1 cup yellow cornmeal
1 cup whole meal flour
1/4 cup demerara sugar
1/4 cup melted butter
1 tablespoon natural yoghurt
1 tablespoon baking powder
1 cup milk
1 beaten egg
1 teaspoon salt
1 teaspoon cinnamon

1. Mix all dry ingredients together in a bowl
2. Make a well in the centre of the dry ingredients and pour the beaten egg into the centre of the dry ingredients
3. Add the milk and beat for a minute
4. Fold in the melted butter then pour the mixture into a greased baking bread tin
5. Bake in a hot oven at 200 degrees Celsius for 30 mins or until when a skewer is placed into mixture it comes out clean

I have always encouraged myself just as David encouraged himself in the Lord even as I write this book. Please be mindful that your gift comes naturally to you, it is your passion and it will bring you before great men and this is what "My Gift of Hospitality" has done for me.

My prayer is:

May the favour of the Lord our God rest on us; and establish the work of our hands. Psalm 90:17.

Then we can boldly declare surely goodness and mercy shall follow us all the days in our lives and we will dwell in the house of the Lord forever and ever Psalm 23:6

In Conclusion

I hope this book will enhance your Gastronomic Experience and will encourage you to be part of our Ghanaian Hospitality journey and then you may consider to visit Ghana, My Motherland.

9 781490 794167